No-Fuss DINNER PARTIES

Some of the best meals are the ones you enjoy with friends, and whether these result from a last minute invitation or are carefully planned well in advance, the outcome should be the same: great food, companionship, relaxation and laughter.

No-Fuss Dinner Parties *contains all the recipes you would choose for easy entertaining. Soups that are sufficiently out-of-the-ordinary to provide a stimulating start to a meal, but which are simple to prepare and absolutely delicious; starters which take only minutes to make but which appear to be the result of hours of loving labour; dinners for drop-in guests, more elaborate special occasion dishes and simply sumptuous sweets.*

There's even a selection of cocktails and alcohol-free drinks. Finally, for the easiest ever dinner dates, turn to the chapter of the same name. There you'll find menus for all sorts of special occasions, from Sunday lunch to a bother-free barbecue, plus a vegetarian menu that is sure to find favour. All the menus have been selected for ease of preparation and include cook-ahead starters and desserts, fresh ideas for salads and vegetables and suggestions for alternative dishes.

CONTENTS

COME TO LUNCH	3
STAY FOR DINNER	11
DINNER DATES	21
DROP IN FOR DRINKS	36
COME AGAIN	42
INDEX	48

COME TO LUNCH

What could be better on a chilly winter's day than a bowl of satisfying soup served with crusty bread? This chapter offers a selection, from a hearty vegetable soup to more adventurous combinations of fish and shellfish. Summer guests will be spoiled for choice with super salads, speedy grills and filo parcels.

Italian Mussel Soup

60ml (2fl oz) sunflower oil

1 clove garlic, crushed

1 x 397g (13oz) can chopped tomatoes

600ml (1pt) passata (puréed tomatoes)

60ml (2fl oz) white wine

1 tblspn snipped fresh basil, plus extra to garnish

24 mussels, scrubbed and bearded

60ml (2fl oz) single cream

1 Heat the oil in a large saucepan over gentle heat. Add the garlic and sauté for 2 minutes. Stir in the tomatoes, passata, wine and basil. Simmer for 15 minutes.

2 Add the mussels, discarding any whose shells are open and which do not snap shut when tapped. Cover the pan, raise the heat to high and steam the mussels for about 5 minutes or until the shells open.

3 Transfer the mussels to a bowl, remove them from the shells and return them to the soup. Stir in the cream and serve, garnished with snipped fresh basil.
Serves 4

Scallop Soup with Vermouth and Lime

185g (6oz) scallops, rinsed and deveined

1 spring onion, cut into matchstick strips

1 carrot, cut into matchstick strips

1 litre (1³/₄pt) chicken stock

4 slices fresh root ginger

5 tblspn dry vermouth

salt

freshly ground black pepper

1 lime, very thinly sliced, for garnish

1 Place the scallops in the freezer for 1 hour. Cut into very thin strips. Set the scallops, spring onion and carrot aside in individual bowls.

2 Combine the stock and ginger in a saucepan. Bring to the boil, lower the heat and stir in the vermouth. Simmer for 5 minutes. Using a slotted spoon, remove and discard the ginger.

3 Add the carrot strips to the pan and cook for 2 minutes. Add the scallops and cook for 30 seconds, then add the spring onion and cook for 1 minute more.

4 Remove the soup from the heat, stir in salt and pepper to taste and serve at once in heated bowls. Float thin slices of lime on each portion.
Serves 4

Italian Mussel Soup

Smoked Salmon Soup

750ml (1¹/₄pt) fish stock, see Kitchen Tip, page 15

125ml (4fl oz) single cream

250ml (8fl oz) milk

¹/₂ tspn grated nutmeg

salt

freshly ground black pepper

100g (3¹/₂oz) smoked salmon, cut into thin strips

snipped chives for garnish

Bring stock to boil. Lower heat and stir in cream, milk and nutmeg, season to taste. Set aside salmon for garnish, add rest to soup. Heat through gently without boiling. Serve in heated bowls, garnished with reserved salmon and chives.

Serves 4

Winter Vegetable Soup

75g (2¹/₂oz) butter

4 leeks, washed and sliced

2 cloves garlic, finely chopped

2 parsnips, sliced

2 carrots, sliced

1 large celeriac, chopped

3 large potatoes, chopped

1 turnip, chopped

1 swede (¹/₂ if large), chopped

1.5 litres (2¹/₂pt) chicken stock

1 x 440g (14oz) can butterbeans, drained

salt

freshly ground black pepper

chopped fresh dill to garnish

1 Melt butter in saucepan. Cook leeks and garlic over gentle heat for 5 minutes, without browning.

2 Add parsnips, carrots, celeriac, potatoes, turnip and swede, with chicken stock. Bring to boil, lower heat and simmer for 20 minutes. Stir in beans and simmer for 10 minutes more or until all the vegetables are soft. Purée in a blender or food processor until smooth.

3 Return soup to clean pan and heat through. Season to taste. Serve very hot, garnished with dill.

Serves 6

Watercress Soup

2 bunches watercress, thoroughly washed

60g (2oz) butter

1 leek, chopped

1 large potato, diced

1.5 litres (2¹/₂pt) chicken stock

salt

pinch grated nutmeg

250ml (8fl oz) single cream

1 Set aside 6 watercress sprigs for garnish. Cut rest into short lengths, discarding any tough stems.

2 Melt butter in a large saucepan. Add leek and potato. Sauté over gentle heat for about 10 minutes until the vegetables are softened but not browned.

3 Add stock. Bring to boil, lower heat and simmer for 10 minutes. Add watercress with salt to taste (see Kitchen Tip). Stir in nutmeg and simmer for 5 minutes more.

4 Purée soup in a blender or food processor. Return to saucepan, adjust seasoning if necessary and stir in cream. Reheat over gentle heat without boiling. Serve in heated bowls, garnished with the reserved watercress sprigs.

Serves 6

Kitchen Tip

Watercress has a naturally peppery flavour, so the soup is unlikely to need additional pepper.

Smoked Salmon Soup

Spinach Soup with Sausage Meatballs

Spinach Soup with Sausage Meatballs

250ml (8fl oz) dry white wine

750ml (1¼pt) chicken stock

250g (8oz) drained canned tomatoes, chopped

2 spring onions, finely sliced

2 tblspn tomato purée

350g (11oz) pork sausagemeat

2 tspn dried mixed herbs (optional)

100g (3½oz) large mushrooms, sliced

2 drained canned pimientos, thinly sliced

125g (4oz) fresh leaf spinach, shredded

1 In a saucepan boil wine until reduced by half. Lower heat and add stock, tomatoes, spring onions and tomato purée. Bring to boil, lower heat and simmer for 1 minute.

2 Roll sausagemeat into small balls, adding herbs, if liked. Add them to soup and cook for 7 minutes.

3 Stir in mushrooms, pimientos and spinach. Cook for 3 minutes. Serve in heated bowls.
Serves 4

Mozzarella Ham Parcels

200g (6½oz) mozzarella cheese

4 square slices cooked ham

4 spring onions

12 sun-dried tomatoes

125g (4oz) stuffed green olives

rocket or radicchio lettuce (optional)

1 clove garlic, crushed

125ml (4fl oz) olive oil

1 tblspn chopped fresh basil

1 tspn crushed black peppercorns

1 tblspn lemon juice

1 Cut mozzarella into four 2cm (¾in) wide sticks, a little longer than width of ham. Roll each mozzarella stick in a ham slice and tie a spring onion around each parcel.

2 Place on individual plates, arrange sun-dried tomatoes and olives around them. Add a little rocket or radicchio if liked.

3 Mix remaining ingredients in a screwtop jar, close lid tightly and shake until well mixed. Drizzle over salad garnish and serve.
Serves 4

Pear and Smoked Chicken Salad

2 ripe pears

375g (12oz) smoked chicken or turkey, skinned and cut in strips

30g (1oz) butter

1 bunch watercress

4 spring onions, finely chopped

1 clove garlic, crushed

2 tspn tarragon vinegar

1 tblspn dry white wine

250ml (8fl oz) double cream

1 Trim the pears, slice them in half lengthwise and remove the cores. Place each pear half, skin side up, on a board. Cut lengthwise into slices, keeping the pear connected at the stem end, and fan out on individual plates, as illustrated right. Arrange a pile of smoked chicken or turkey strips beside each fanned pear.

2 Make the sauce. Melt the butter in a saucepan. Reserve 4 watercress sprigs for garnish. Chop the rest, discarding any tough stalks. Add the watercress, spring onions, garlic, vinegar and white wine to the melted butter and simmer for 5 minutes.

3 Stir in the cream and simmer, uncovered, for 10 minutes or until the sauce has thickened. Purée the sauce in a blender or food processor, spoon a little over each pear half and serve.

Serves 4

Pear and Smoked Chicken Salad

Cold Garlic Prawns with Avocado

2 ripe avocados, halved, stoned and peeled

500g (1lb) peeled cooked prawns, deveined, tails intact

1 large onion, cut into thin rings

3 cloves garlic, crushed

2 tblspn olive oil

60ml (2fl oz) lemon juice

30ml (1fl oz) white wine vinegar

1 tblspn chopped fresh parsley

1 Slice the avocados neatly and arrange on a serving platter with the prawns and onion rings.

2 Whisk the garlic, olive oil, lemon juice and vinegar in a small bowl, pour over the salad and sprinkle with parsley. Serve.

Serves 4

Cold Garlic Prawns with Avocado, Seafood Terrine

Seafood Terrine

500g (1lb) white fish fillets, skinned

2 egg whites

375ml (12fl oz) double cream

2 tblspn lemon juice

250g (8oz) shelled cooked prawns, chopped

3 large courgettes, thinly sliced

1 lemon, quartered, optional

selection fresh herbs, optional

1 Cut the fish into small pieces, removing any remaining bones; purée in a blender or food processor. Press the purée through a sieve into a bowl.

2 Set the bowl over ice, add the egg whites and cream and beat the mixture with a wooden spoon until thick. Beat in the lemon juice.

3 Brush a loaf tin with oil, line with baking parchment and brush with oil again.

4 Spoon half the fish purée into a separate bowl and add the prawns. Spread half the plain fish purée over the base of the loaf tin, arrange half the courgette slices on top, then spread half the prawn mixture over the courgettes.

5 Add a second layer of courgette slices followed by the rest of the prawn mixture. Spread the rest of the plain fish purée on top, cover the terrine with foil and place in a roasting tin. Add boiling water to come halfway up the sides of the terrine.

6 Bake for 30 minutes. Leave the terrine to cool in the tin for 10 minutes before turning out. Garnish with lemon quarters and fresh herbs, if liked.

Serves 6-8

Chicken Breasts with Lemon and Brandy

60g (2oz) plain flour
1 tblspn finely snipped chives
salt
freshly ground black pepper
6 skinless chicken breast fillets
155g (5oz) butter
5 tblspn lemon juice
5 tblspn brandy
3 tblspn chopped fresh parsley

1 Combine flour, chives, salt and pepper in a deep plate. Dredge chicken in seasoned flour, shaking off the excess.

2 Melt half butter in a large heavy-based frying pan until foaming. Add chicken and sauté for 4 minutes on each side.

3 Stir lemon juice into pan juices. Heat brandy in a metal soup ladle, ignite it carefully and pour it over chicken. When flames subside, transfer chicken to a heated platter and keep hot.

4 Whisk remaining butter into sauce, 1 tablespoon at a time. Pour over chicken, sprinkle with parsley and serve at once.
Serves 4

Chicken and Mushroom Parcels

60g (2oz) butter
4 skinless chicken breast fillets
375g (12oz) mushrooms, sliced
4 large rounds thinly sliced cooked ham
12 sheets filo pastry
125ml (4fl oz) oil

1 Preheat oven to 180°C (350°F/ Gas 4). Melt butter in a large frying pan over moderate heat. Add chicken fillets and mush-rooms. Fry for 8 minutes, stirring occasionally and turning chicken fillets over halfway through cooking. Drain the chicken and mushrooms on paper towels.

2 Place a chicken fillet on each slice of ham. Top with a quarter of mushrooms and bring up ham to make a parcel.

3 Brush a sheet of filo with a little of oil. Top with a second sheet of filo, brush with oil again and repeat process with a third filo sheet. Place one of ham-wrapped chicken parcels in centre of layered filo; wrap neatly to make a pillow shape. Wrap remaining chicken portions in same way.

4 Place chicken and mushroom parcels on greased baking sheets. Bake for 30 minutes. Serve at once, with a green salad and cherry tomatoes tossed in basil vinaigrette.
Serves 4

Kitchen Tip
While working with the first three filo sheets, keep the remainder covered with a clean tea-towel to prevent them from drying out.

Peppered Chicken Breast Fillets

4 skinless chicken breast fillets
2 tblspn cracked black pepper
60g (2oz) butter
125ml (4fl oz) Madeira
250ml (8fl oz) single cream

1 Preheat oven to 150°C (300°F/ Gas 2). Sprinkle both sides of each chicken fillet with pepper, pressing it well into the chicken.

2 Melt butter in a large frying pan over moderate heat. Add the chicken breasts. Fry chicken, turning once, until just tender. Transfer to an ovenproof dish and keep warm in the oven.

3 Add Madeira and cream to fat remaining in frying pan. Bring to boil, lower heat and simmer sauce until reduced by half. Pour over chicken. Serve at once, with steamed green beans and grilled tomatoes, if liked.
Serves 4

Peppered Chicken Breast Fillets

STAY FOR DINNER

When friends drop in unexpectedly, 'stay for dinner' can be a very welcome invitation. Under these circumstances, the cook needs a repertoire of simple dishes that can either be thrown together and largely ignored, or cooked at the last minute, preferably using ingredients from pantry, freezer or corner shop.

Glazed Ham and Sausagemeat Loaf

This delicous loaf is easy to make, versatile and relatively inexpensive, particularly if you use ham offcuts. Substitute dried breadcrumbs and chopped fresh parsley for the stuffing mix if preferred.

375g (12oz) lean cooked ham

90g (3oz) no-need-to-soak dried apricots

500g (1lb) pork sausagemeat

1 x 114g (3¹/₂oz) packet apple and herb stuffing mix

300ml (10fl oz) milk

90g (3oz) soft brown sugar

3 tblspn apple cider vinegar

2 tblspn Dijon mustard

60ml (2fl oz) water

1 Preheat oven to 180°C (350°F/ Gas 4). Finely chop ham and apricots together in a food processor or by hand.

2 Put sausagemeat in a mixing bowl, add ham mixture and stuffing mix and mix well with clean hands. Stir in milk.

3 Spoon mixture into a large greased and lined loaf tin. Bake for 30 minutes.

4 Meanwhile bring remaining ingredients to boil in a small saucepan. Simmer until syrupy.

5 Brush top of loaf with some of the glaze. Bake for 30 minutes more, brushing loaf with glaze every 10 minutes.

6 Turn loaf out on a baking sheet, remove lining paper and brush with remaining glaze. Bake for 15 minutes more. Garnish with orange slices and watercress, if liked. Serve hot or cold.
Serves 6-8

Prawns with Garlic and Rosemary

500g (1lb) uncooked king prawns, peeled and deveined

2 cloves garlic, crushed

3 tblspn olive oil

¹/₄ tspn freshly ground black pepper

2 fresh rosemary sprigs

45g (1¹/₂oz) butter

125ml (4fl oz) dry vermouth

1 Combine prawns, garlic, olive oil, pepper and rosemary in a large bowl; toss well. Cover bowl and marinate in refrigerator for 8 hours or overnight.

2 Melt butter in a large frying pan. Add prawns, with marinade, and shake pan over high heat for about 2 minutes or until prawns are pink.

3 Using a slotted spoon, transfer prawns to a bowl. Discard the rosemary. Stir vermouth into frying pan, bring to boil and cook until reduced to a moderately thick glaze.

4 Return prawns to pan and toss in glaze. Spoon onto a heated serving dish and serve.
Serves 4

Glazed Ham and Sausagemeat Loaf

Risotto with Smoked Salmon

Risotto with Smoked Salmon

3 tblspn olive oil

2 onions, chopped

2 cloves garlic, crushed

1/4 tspn ground turmeric

1 red pepper, diced

315g (10oz) risotto rice

750ml (1¼pt) fish or chicken stock

2 tblspn chopped spring onions

1 tblspn chopped fresh basil

1 tblspn snipped chives

125g (4oz) smoked salmon, cut into strips

1 Heat oil in a large frying pan. Add onions, garlic and turmeric and cook for 2 minutes, stirring frequently. Add pepper and cook for 5 minutes.

2 Sprinkle rice over vegetables. Add stock and bring to boil. Lower heat and simmer, uncovered, for 20 minutes or until rice is tender and most of liquid has been absorbed.

3 Stir in remaining ingredients. Serve hot or cold.

Serves 4

Tomato Pilaf

60ml (2fl oz) olive oil

1 onion, chopped

250g (8oz) ripe tomatoes, peeled and chopped

440ml (14fl oz) chicken stock

2 tspn tomato purée

1 tspn sugar

pinch each of allspice and cinnamon

salt

freshly ground black pepper

250g (8oz) long grain rice

3 tblspn chopped fresh parsley

1 Heat oil in a heavy-based saucepan. Add onion and sauté for about 5 minutes, until golden. Stir in tomatoes. Simmer, uncovered, for about 10 minutes to create a thick sauce.

2 Add stock, tomato purée, sugar and spices, with salt and pepper to taste. Bring to boil and stir in rice. Allow mixture to return to boil.

3 Stir mixture, then cover pan, lower heat and simmer for about 18 minutes or until liquid has been absorbed and rice is tender.

4 Off heat, lift pan lid and place several paper towels above rice mixture to absorb steam. Leave for 5 minutes. Fluff rice with a fork, sprinkle with parsley and serve.

Serves 4

Risotto with Cheese and Pinenuts

60g (2oz) butter

1 onion, finely chopped

375g (12oz) brown rice

1 litre (1¾pt) chicken stock

30g (1oz) pinenuts

30g (1oz) Parmesan cheese, grated

1 Melt 45g (1½oz) of butter in a saucepan. Fry onion until golden, then add rice and cook for 3 minutes, stirring.

2 Add 125ml (4fl oz) of stock. Stir mixture constantly, gradually adding more stock.

3 Toast pinenuts under a pre-heated grill. When rice is tender and all stock has been absorbed, stir in remaining butter, in small pieces, with pinenuts and cheese. Serve.

Serves 4

Cheesy Rice Ring with Garlic Vegetables

315g (10oz) cooked long grain white rice

60g (2oz) Parmesan cheese, finely grated

2 tblspn olive oil

3 cloves garlic, crushed

1 red pepper, cut into 1cm (1/2in) squares

1 green pepper, cut into 1cm (1/2in) squares

125g (4oz) oyster mushrooms, sliced

1 tblspn chopped fresh parsley

1 Preheat oven to 180°C (350°F/ Gas 4). Place the cooked rice in a large mixing bowl. Stir in the cheese with 1 tablespoon of the olive oil; mix well. Spoon the rice mixture into a lightly oiled ring mould and press down firmly.

2 Cover the top of the mould with foil. Bake for 10 minutes.

3 Heat the remaining olive oil in a frying pan. Add the garlic and cook over gentle heat for 3 minutes. Add the red and green pepper squares with the mushrooms. Cook, stirring constantly, for 4 minutes. Stir in the parsley.

4 Turn the rice ring out on to a serving plate, fill the centre with the garlic-flavoured vegetables and serve at once.

Serves 4

Variations

Make the ratatouille as in the recipe for Ratatouille Crumble on page 25, omitting the topping. Spoon the ratatouille mixture into the centre of the rice ring and serve.

For a tomato filling, fry 1 chopped onion and 2 crushed garlic cloves in 2 tablespoons olive oil. Add 1 x 397g (13oz) can chopped tomatoes with herbs and 1 teaspoon tomato purée. Bring the mixture to the boil, stirring, then lower the heat and simmer for 10-15 minutes until thick and well-flavoured.

Quick Nasi Goreng

Frozen cooked rice is a great standby. This recipe illustrates how the addition of a few choice ingredients can quickly transform it to a tasty supper dish for unexpected guests.

30g (1oz) butter

3 eggs, beaten

3 tblspn olive oil

6 rindless streaky bacon rashers, chopped

1 clove garlic, crushed

500g (1lb) uncooked prawns, peeled and deveined, cut into 1cm (1/2in) lengths

1 onion, chopped

2 tblspn soy sauce

500g (1lb) cooked long grain white rice

1/4 cucumber, diced

3 tblspn sultanas

2 tblspn chopped fresh parsley

1 Heat the butter in an omelette pan over moderate heat. Add the beaten eggs, tilting the pan to spread the mixture evenly. Cook until the underside of the omelette is lightly browned. Transfer to a plate and set aside.

2 Add the oil to the frying pan and heat. Fry the bacon, garlic, prawns and onion for 3 minutes, then transfer to a bowl, using a slotted spoon.

3 Stir the soy sauce, rice, cucumber and sultanas into the oil remaining in the pan. Cook for 2 minutes, then return the prawn mixture to the pan and cook for 1 minute more.

4 Roll up the omelette, cut it into thin strips and add to the frying pan. Toss lightly, stir in the parsley and serve.

Serves 4

Quick Nasi Goreng

Seafood Pot Pie

The pastry crust on this popular pie hides a delicious filling of scallops, prawns and vegetables in a creamy sauce.

500ml (16fl oz) dry white wine

500g (1lb) scallops, rinsed and deveined

45g (1½oz) butter

1 dessert apple, peeled, cored and chopped

1 onion, chopped

1 large carrot, chopped

½ red pepper, chopped

125ml (4fl oz) chicken stock

125ml (4fl oz) single cream

2 tblspn cornflour

60ml (2fl oz) milk

375g (12oz) uncooked prawns, peeled and deveined

90g (3oz) thawed frozen or drained canned sweetcorn

1 x 215g (7½oz) packet frozen puff pastry, thawed

1 egg, beaten, to glaze

1 Preheat oven to 180°C (350°F/ Gas 4). Bring wine to boil in a large deep frying pan. Cook until reduced by one third. Add scallops, lower heat and simmer until just opaque. Using a slotted spoon, transfer scallops to a bowl and set aside. Reserve reduced wine stock.

2 Melt butter in a large saucepan over moderate heat. Add apple, onion, carrot and red pepper and sauté for 5 minutes.

3 Pour in reserved wine stock, with chicken stock and cream. Bring mixture to boil, lower heat and simmer for 5 minutes.

4 In a cup or small bowl, mix cornflour to a smooth paste with milk. Stir paste into simmering mixture. Cook over moderate heat, stirring, until sauce thickens.

5 Stir in reserved scallops with prawns and corn. Pour mixture into a 23cm (9in) pie dish.

6 Roll out pastry on a lightly floured surface to fit top of pie. Knock up the sides and scallop edges if liked. Make a few slits in pastry, decorate with pastry trimmings and glaze with beaten egg. Bake for 30 minutes or until the crust is risen and golden. Serve at once.
Serves 4

Spanish Seafood Casserole

1 frozen uncooked lobster tail, thawed

2 tblspn oil

2 onions, chopped

1 small green pepper, chopped

1 small red pepper, chopped

2 cloves garlic, crushed

2 tomatoes, chopped

250ml (8fl oz) water

125ml (4fl oz) dry white wine

5 tblspn brandy

2 tblspn lemon juice

pinch powdered saffron

2 bay leaves

500g (1lb) uncooked king prawns in shells

500g (1lb) mussels, scrubbed and bearded

2 tblspn chopped fresh parsley

1 Cut lobster meat into large chunks. Heat oil in a large saucepan. Stir fry onions, peppers and garlic for 2 minutes, then add tomatoes and cook for 5 minutes more. Stir in water, wine, brandy, lemon juice, saffron and bay leaves. Bring to boil, then simmer for 1 minute.

2 Add lobster, prawns and mussels. Cook over gentle heat until all mussels have opened and shellfish is tender. Discard any mussels that remain closed. Serve at once, garnished with parsley.
Serves 4

Spanish Seafood Casserole

Lemon Sole Ragout

45g (1¹/₂oz) butter

2 green peppers, sliced into thin strips

2 red peppers, sliced into thin strips

1 large onion, thinly sliced

2 cloves garlic, crushed

3 tomatoes, chopped

3 tblspn finely chopped fresh parsley

1 tspn chopped fresh thyme

¹/₂ red chilli, seeded and finely chopped

250ml (8fl oz) fish stock, see Kitchen Tip

125ml (4fl oz) dry white wine

250g (8oz) potatoes, cut into 1cm (¹/₂in) slices

salt

freshly ground black pepper

750g (1¹/₂lb) lemon sole or plaice fillets, skinned

1 Melt butter in a heavy-based saucepan and cook peppers, onion and garlic until softened. Add tomatoes, parsley, thyme, chilli, fish stock and wine; mix well.

2 Arrange potatoes on top of the mixture. Season with salt and pepper. Bring liquid to boil, lower heat, simmer and cook until potatoes are tender when pierced with a skewer.

3 Place fish fillets on top of the potatoes. Add salt and pepper to taste, cover the pan and simmer briefly until fish is cooked. Remove fish and keep hot.

4 Spoon mixed vegetables and potatoes onto heated plates, top with fish fillets and serve.

Serves 6

Kitchen Tip
To make fish stock, put the fish trimmings in a saucepan (avoiding the gills, which will make the stock bitter). Add ¹/₂ onion, 1 sliced celery stick, 4 white peppercorns, ¹/₂ tspn salt and a bouquet garni. Add 600ml (1pt) water. Bring to the boil, simmer for 30 minutes, strain and use.

Fennel with Ham

60g (2oz) butter

1 onion, chopped

185g (6oz) cooked ham, chopped

4 fennel bulbs, trimmed and cut into wedges

500ml (16fl oz) chicken stock

salt

freshly ground black pepper

60g (2oz) Parmesan cheese, grated

1 Melt butter in a large frying pan. Sauté onion until golden. Add ham and fennel. Cook over low heat for 10 minutes, stirring occasionally.

2 Add chicken stock, raise heat and cook mixture until stock has evaporated to leave a glaze on the fennel. Add salt and pepper to taste.

3 Sprinkle with Parmesan, toss quickly and serve at once.
Serves 4

Pork with Apple Cider Sauce

2 tblspn olive oil

1 onion, sliced

2 Granny Smith apples, peeled and sliced

250ml (8fl oz) dry apple cider

1 tblspn pitted prunes, chopped

1 tblspn lemon juice

500g (1lb) pork fillets, trimmed

1 tblspn chopped fresh parsley

1 Preheat oven to 180°C (350°F/ Gas 4). Heat oil in a saucepan. Add onion and apples and cook for 5 minutes, stirring.

2 Add cider and prunes. Bring to boil, lower heat and simmer for 5 minutes. Add lemon juice.

3 Arrange pork fillets in a lightly greased shallow ovenproof dish. Pour apple mixture over and around pork. Bake for about 45 minutes or until pork is cooked. Serve at once, sprinkled with parsley.
Serves 4

Apricot Chicken

6 chicken breast fillets

300ml (10fl oz) apricot nectar

4 spring onions, chopped

2 tspn wholegrain mustard

1 clove garlic, crushed

60g (2oz) flaked almonds, toasted

1 Preheat oven to 180°C (350°F/ Gas 4). Arrange chicken fillets in a lightly greased shallow ovenproof dish.

2 Combine apricot nectar, spring onions, mustard and garlic in a bowl. Pour mixture over chicken. Turn chicken to coat fillets thoroughly.

3 Bake for about 30 minutes or until chicken is cooked through. Garnish with almonds and serve.
Serves 6

Orange-scented Oxtail Stew

1 tblspn olive oil

1.25kg (2½lb) oxtail, cut into thick sections, trimmed

3 cloves garlic, finely chopped

250ml (8fl oz) orange juice

1 tblspn finely grated orange rind

1 tblspn cornflour

125ml (4fl oz) beef stock

1 tblspn orange marmalade

1 tblspn Worcestershire sauce

1 tspn crushed black peppercorns

2 oranges, peeled and segmented

2 tblspn finely chopped spring onions

1 Heat oil in a saucepan, add oxtail, garlic, orange juice and rind. Cook, for 5 minutes. Pour over water to cover, lower heat, cover and simmer for 2 hours, skimming surface occasionally and topping up water as required.

2 Transfer oxtail to a bowl. When cool, cover and refrigerate. Boil liquid in pan, if necessary, until reduced to about 1.2 litres (2pt). Pour into a bowl. When cool,

refrigerate until fat sets on top; discard.

3 Return degreased liquid and oxtail to clean pan. Mix cornflour with stock in a bowl. Stir in orange marmalade and Worcester-shire sauce. Add contents of bowl to pan and cook for 30 minutes or until oxtail is very tender. To serve, stir in crushed pepper, orange segments and spring onions.
Serves 4-6

Pork and Mushroom Casserole

2 tblspn olive oil

2 onions, chopped

4 rindless streaky bacon rashers, chopped

2 cloves garlic, crushed

1kg (2lb) lean pork, trimmed and cubed

470ml (15fl oz) chicken stock

155ml (5fl oz) white wine

30g (1oz) butter

375g (12oz) mushrooms, halved if large

30g (1oz) plain flour

300ml (10floz) single cream

¼ tspn cayenne pepper

salt

freshly ground black pepper

1 Preheat oven to 180°C (350°F/ Gas 4). Heat oil in a flameproof casserole. Add onions, bacon and garlic and stir fry for 5 minutes. Add pork and stir fry until browned. Drain off excess oil. Pour over stock and wine; mix well. Bake, covered, for 1 hour, stirring occasionally.

2 Melt butter in a frying pan, add mushrooms and cook for 5 minutes. Stir in flour and cook for 1 minute. Gradually add cream, stirring until mixture boils and thickens. Stir in cayenne, season to taste.

3 Stir mixture into the casserole, return to oven and cook for 15 minutes or until heated through. Stir again just before serving.
Serves 6

Pork and Mushroom Casserole, Orange-scented Oxtail Stew

Linguine with Prawns and Olives

315g (10oz) linguine

60g (2oz) butter

2 cloves garlic, crushed

1 large onion, chopped

60g (2oz) pitted black olives, chopped

2 x 397g (13oz) cans chopped tomatoes

1 tspn sugar

1 tblspn tomato purée

2 tspn dried rosemary, crumbled

315g (10oz) uncooked prawns, peeled and deveined, tails intact

30g (1oz) Parmesan cheese, grated

2 tblspn chopped fresh parsley

1 Bring a saucepan of lightly salted water to boil. Add the linguine and cook until just tender. Drain and set aside.

2 Melt butter, add garlic, onion and olives, cook for 3 minutes. Add tomatoes, sugar, tomato purée and rosemary. Cook for 5 minutes. Add prawns and cook for 3 minutes. Add linguine and toss over heat until heated through. Serve dusted with Parmesan and parsley.

Serves 4

Radicchio with Peas

375g (12oz) frozen peas, thawed

30g (1oz) butter

2 tblspn clear honey

1 tblspn lemon juice

8 radicchio leaves, shredded

1 Bring a large saucepan of lightly salted water to boil. Cook peas for 2 minutes. Drain, refresh under cold running water and drain again.

2 Melt butter in saucepan. Stir in honey and lemon juice. Cook for 1 minute. Mix peas and radicchio in a bowl, add honey butter, toss and serve at once.

Serves 4

Radicchio with Peas, Linguine with Prawns and Olives

Wholemeal Pasta with Mushrooms and Sun-dried Tomatoes

Wholemeal Pasta with Mushrooms and Sun-dried Tomatoes

410g (13oz) wholemeal penne or macaroni

1 tblspn olive oil

2 cloves garlic, crushed

125g (4oz) button mushrooms, halved if large

60g (2oz) sun-dried tomatoes, cut into strips

2 tblspn chopped fresh basil

1 Bring a large saucepan of lightly salted water to boil. Add pasta and cook until just tender. Drain and set aside.

2 Heat oil in a large frying pan. Add garlic, mushrooms and sun-dried tomatoes; cook for 2 minutes.

3 Stir in basil and pasta. Toss until heated through. Serve.

Serves 4

Fettucine Alfredo

60g (2oz) butter

250ml (8fl oz) single cream

125g (4oz) Parmesan cheese, grated

salt

500g (1lb) fettucine

freshly ground black pepper

1 Melt butter in a large saucepan. Add cream and Parmesan. Heat through but do not allow sauce to boil.

2 Bring a large saucepan of lightly salted water to the boil. Add fettucine and cook until just tender. Drain, add to cream sauce and toss over low heat until heated through. Serve hot with plenty of black pepper.

Serves 4

DINNER DATES

Celebrations call for special meals, and what better way to mark an occasion than with a dinner for friends? This chapter offers a selection of menus, each one planned to make entertaining as easy and enjoyable as possible.

ANNIVERSARY MENU

Warm Mussel Salad with Walnut Dressing

Lamb in Red Wine

Rosemary Crispy Potatoes

Glazed Turnips and Carrots

Berries and Mascarpone

Warm Mussel Salad with Walnut Dressing

If the lettuce leaves are washed, dried and stored in a polythene bag in the refrigerator, the salad can be completed in minutes.

assorted lettuce leaves
small bunch watercress
375ml (12fl oz) dry white wine
4 spring onions, finely chopped
125ml (4fl oz) water
16 mussels, scrubbed and bearded
60ml (2fl oz) walnut oil
sliced spring onion green and halved
walnuts for garnish

1 Wash and dry lettuce leaves. Arrange them decoratively with watercress on individual plates.

2 Bring wine to boil in a medium saucepan. Stir in spring onions with the water.

3 Add mussels, discarding any with open shells which do not snap shut when tapped. Cover pan, raise heat to high and steam mussels for about 5 minutes or until shells open.

4 Drain mussels, discarding any whose shells remain shut; reserve cooking liquid. Arrange mussels on their half shells on the lettuce mixture.

5 Whisk 4 tablespoons of the reserved cooking liquid with oil; dress salad. Garnish and serve at once.
Serves 4

Warm Mussel Salad with Walnut Dressing

Lamb in Red Wine

Lamb in Red Wine

2 tblspn oil

4 rindless streaky bacon rashers, chopped

1kg (2lb) lean boneless lamb, cut into bite-size cubes

2 onions, chopped

750ml (1¹/₄pt) lamb or chicken stock

375ml (12fl oz) red wine

2 tblspn tomato purée

1 tblspn Worcestershire sauce

1 tblspn fruit chutney

4 tblspn cornflour dissolved in 6 tblspn cold water

4 tblspn chopped fresh parsley

1 Preheat oven to 180°C (350°F/ Gas 4). Heat oil in a flameproof casserole and fry bacon, lamb and onions until well browned, stirring constantly. Drain off excess oil.

2 Combine stock, wine, tomato purée, worcestershire sauce and chutney in a bowl. Stir mixture into dish. Add cornflour mixture and half parsley and stir well.

3 Bake for 2 hours or until lamb is tender, stirring occasionally. Sprinkle remaining parsley over the top when serving.
Serves 4

Rosemary Crispy Potatoes

750g (1¹/₂lb) potatoes

1 bunch spring onions, chopped

1 tblspn chopped fresh rosemary

salt

freshly ground black pepper

1 tspn sunflower oil

5 tblspn chicken stock

rosemary sprigs for garnish

1 Preheat oven to 200°C (400°F/ Gas 6). Cook potatoes in a saucepan of lightly salted boiling water until tender. Drain. When cool, cut into 2cm (³/₄in) cubes.

2 Combine potatoes, spring onions and rosemary in a bowl. Add a little salt and plenty of pepper. Toss well.

3 Brush a baking dish with oil. Add potato mixture and pour over chicken stock.

4 Bake on a high shelf for about 50 minutes, stirring every 15 minutes so that potatoes brown evenly. Garnish and serve.
Serves 4

Glazed Turnips and Carrots

30g (1oz) butter

2 tblspn clear honey

1 tspn soft brown sugar

2 tspn lemon juice

3 turnips, finely sliced

3 large carrots, finely sliced

1 tblspn snipped fresh mint

1 Combine butter, honey, sugar and lemon juice in a shallow frying pan. Place over moderate heat, stirring occasionally, until butter, honey and sugar have melted to form a smooth sauce.

2 Slowly bring mixture to the boil, lower heat and add turnip and carrot slices. Cook, turning frequently, for about 8 minutes or until vegetables are cooked and sauce has reduced to a glaze. Transfer to a heated platter, decorate with mint strips and serve.

Serves 4

Glazed Turnips and Carrots

Berries and Mascarpone

500g (1lb) blueberries or raspberries

250g (8oz) strawberries, hulled and quartered

2 tblspn brandy

1 tblspn clear honey

2 tblspn freshly squeezed lime juice

4 tblspn freshly squeezed orange juice

200g (6¹/₂oz) mascarpone

broken caramel pieces for decoration (optional)

1 Place blueberries or raspberries in bottom of 4 serving dishes. Top with strawberries.

2 Mix brandy, honey and citrus juices together. Divide mixture between dishes.

3 Spoon mascarpone on top and decorate with caramel, if liked.

Serves 4

Berries and Mascarpone

A varied selection of vegetables are served with this menu to provide vegetarian guests with plenty of choice.

Loin of Lamb with Prune Pinenut Stuffing

60ml (2fl oz) red wine

45g (1¹/₂oz) pitted prunes, chopped

30g (1oz) pinenuts

45g (1¹/₂oz) chopped no-need-to-soak dried apricots

30g (1oz) ground almonds

1 tblspn chopped fresh parsley

750g (1¹/₂lb) boned loin of lamb

1 In a small bowl combine red wine, prunes, pinenuts, apricots, ground almonds and parsley. Mix well, cover and set aside for 30 minutes.

2 Preheat oven to 180°C (350°F/ Gas 4). Spoon stuffing along the centre of loin of lamb; wrap up and secure tightly with string.

3 Transfer to a roasting tin and roast for 45 minutes or until cooked as desired.
Serves 4

Loin of Lamb with Prune Pinenut Stuffing served with Ratatouille Crumble

Green Beans with Sesame Seeds

Ratatouille Crumble

60ml (2fl oz) olive oil

2 cloves garlic, crushed

1 onion, chopped

1 red pepper, cut into squares

1 large aubergine, cut into large cubes

1 tblspn tomato purée

3 tblspn white wine

2 tomatoes, cut into large cubes

90g (3oz) dried breadcrumbs

30g (1oz) Parmesan cheese, grated

1 tblspn chopped fresh parsley

60g (2oz) butter, melted

1 Preheat oven to 180°C (350°F/ Gas 4). Heat oil in a large frying pan over moderate heat. Add garlic, onion, red pepper and aubergine and stir fry for 2 minutes.

2 Stir in tomato purée, wine and tomatoes. Cook, stirring frequently, for 10 minutes.

3 Mix breadcrumbs, Parmesan, parsley and melted butter in a separate bowl.

4 Spoon ratatouille into an ovenproof dish. Sprinkle the breadcrumb mixture on top and bake for 20 minutes or until the topping is crisp.
Serves 4

Green Beans with Sesame Seeds

1 tblspn olive oil

1 tblspn sesame seeds

250g (8oz) green beans, trimmed and cut into 3cm (1¹/4in) diagonal pieces

2 tspn soy sauce

Preheat a wok, then add the oil. When hot add the sesame seeds. Stir fry until golden. Add the beans and stir fry for 2 minutes or until bright green. Stir in the soy sauce and serve at once.
Serves 4

Glazed Butternut Squash

Glazed Butternut Squash

1/2 butternut squash

30g (1oz) butter

2 tblspn golden syrup

30g (1oz) fresh wholemeal breadcrumbs

1 Preheat oven to 180°C (350°F/ Gas 4). Cut the squash into 3cm (1¼in) thick slices, leaving the skin on, but removing the seeds.

2 Arrange the squash in a greased baking dish. Cover with foil and bake for 35 minutes.

3 Melt the butter with the syrup in a small saucepan. Stir in the breadcrumbs. Pour the mixture over the squash. Bake, uncovered, for 20 minutes more.
Serves 4

Variation
Sliced pumpkin may be used instead of squash and the slices roasted alongside the lamb. Omit the foil covering, but baste frequently with the pan juices. Squash or pumpkin cooked in this way will not be suitable for vegetarians.

Crispy Fantail Potatoes

These potatoes look as good as they taste and are a perfect foil for the ratatouille.

4 large potatoes, peeled

1 tblspn oil

2 tblspn grated Parmesan cheese

1 Preheat oven to 190°C (375°F/ Gas 5). Cut the potatoes in half lengthwise. Place them, cut side down, on a board. Make vertical cuts in each potato, cutting almost but not quite down to the base.

2 Place the potatoes, flat side down, on baking sheets. Brush generously with oil. Bake for 50 minutes or until the potatoes have puffed up, fanned out and become crisp.

3 Sprinkle the potatoes with the grated Parmesan, return to the oven and bake for 2 minutes more or until the cheese has melted. Serve at once.
Serves 4

Orange Jellies with Fresh Fruit

1 x 11g (⅓oz) sachet gelatine

3 tblspn water

500ml (16fl oz) freshly squeezed orange juice

2 tblspn Cointreau

1 tspn grated orange rind

Decoration

whipped cream

1 strip pared orange rind, cut into fine strips

orange segments

seeded black grapes

mint sprigs

Orange Jellies with Fresh Fruit

1 Sprinkle the gelatine onto the water in a small heatproof bowl. When spongy, place the bowl over simmering water and stir until the gelatine has dissolved.

2 Combine the orange juice, Cointreau, orange rind and dissolved gelatine in a large jug. Pour into 4 lightly oiled individual jelly moulds. Chill until set.

3 Unmould the jellies on dessert plates. Decorate with cream, orange rind, fresh fruit and mint.
Serves 4

Kiwi Fruit Sorbet

Both the desserts suggested for this menu are light and fruity, to balance the hearty main course, and both can be prepared ahead.

6 kiwi fruit, peeled

125g (4oz) sugar

250ml (8fl oz) water

juice of 2 large lemons

1 tspn grated lemon rind

1 Purée the kiwi fruit in a blender or food processor. Set aside.

2 Heat sugar and water in a small saucepan, stirring until the sugar has dissolved. Boil without stirring for 5 minutes, then cool.

3 Combine the kiwi fruit purée with the cooled syrup, lemon juice and rind in an ice cream maker and chill according to instructions. Alternatively, freeze in ice trays. When semi-frozen, beat the mixture in a bowl to break up any large ice crystals. Repeat the process, then freeze in a suitable container until solid.

4 Serve in scoops, with sliced kiwi fruit, if liked.
Serves 4

Basil-scented Prawn Skewers

24 uncooked king prawns, peeled and deveined, shells intact

24 lemon slices

5 tblspn chopped fresh basil

Basil Marinade

185ml (6fl oz) dry white wine

60ml (2fl oz) lemon juice

250ml (8fl oz) olive oil

4 tblspn chopped fresh basil

1 tblspn crushed black peppercorns

1 Spread out the prawns in a single layer in a shallow dish.

2 Combine all the ingredients for the marinade in a screwtop jar. Close lid tightly and shake until well combined. Pour the marinade over the prawns, cover the dish and refrigerate for at least 2 hours (up to 6 hours).

3 Drain the prawns, reserving the marinade, and thread them onto skewers, alternating with slices of lemon. Cook over medium coals, turning occasionally, for about 3 minutes each side. Baste occasionally with the reserved marinade, and turn over once. Serve sprinkled with the basil.
Serves 8

Lamb and Mango Skewers

1kg (2lb) cubed leg lamb

185ml (6fl oz) hoisin sauce

60ml (2fl oz) light soy sauce

60ml (2fl oz) rice wine vinegar

60ml (2fl oz) olive oil

1 tblspn grated fresh root ginger

3 mangoes, peeled and cut into 2cm (3/4in) cubes

1 Trim any fat remaining on lamb cubes. Put cubes in a large bowl. Stir in hoisin sauce, soy sauce, vinegar, oil and ginger. Cover bowl and refrigerate for at least 4 hours, preferably overnight.

2 Drain lamb cubes, reserving the marinade. Thread them on skewers, alternately with mango cubes. Grill over hot coals until tender and golden brown.
Serves 8

Steak and Courgette Burgers

625g (1 1/4lb) minced steak

1 small onion, grated

3 small courgettes, grated

1 tblspn soy sauce

1 tspn sesame oil

1 egg yolk

To Serve

8 wholemeal buns, halved

lettuce leaves

1 tomato, sliced

1 red-skinned onion, thinly sliced

1 Combine the minced steak, onion, courgettes, soy sauce, sesame oil and egg yolk in a bowl. Mix well. Shape into 8 burgers.

2 Grill the burgers over hot coals until well cooked. Serve in the toasted buttered buns, with lettuce, tomato and onion slices.
Serves 8

Lamb and Mango Skewers

Beetroot and Carrot Salad

Crisp Cheese Pitta Wedges

6 pitta breads

125g (4oz) butter, softened

2 cloves garlic, crushed

2 tblspn finely chopped fresh parsley

60g (2oz) Cheddar cheese, grated

60g (2oz) Parmesan cheese, grated

1 Preheat oven to 180°C (350°F/ Gas 4). Cut each pitta bread in half. Separate each half into 2 wedges.

2 Beat butter in a bowl with garlic and parsley. Spread mixture over crumb sides of pitta wedges.

3 Mix cheeses; sprinkle them over buttered wedges. Arrange on baking sheets. Bake for 10 minutes or until crisp. Serve.

Serves 8

Crisp Cheese Pitta Wedges

Beetroot and Carrot Salad

6 small beetroot

6 carrots, sliced in matchsticks

4 tblspn red wine vinegar

2 tblspn lemon juice

4 hard-boiled eggs, sliced, then halved

1 Cook beetroot in boiling water until tender. When cool enough to handle, remove skins. Cool to room temperature; slice into matchstick strips.

2 Combine beetroot and carrot sticks in a bowl. Whisk the vinegar and lemon juice together. Add salt and pepper if required. Toss vegetables lightly in dressing, then arrange on a serving plate with hard-boiled eggs. Garnish with fresh herbs and halved lemon slices, if liked.

Serves 8

VEGETARIAN MENU

*Brie with Raspberry Coulis
and Brioche Toasts*

or

Tomato Picasso

Summer Vegetable Pie

*Parmesan-coated Fried
Fennel*

*Spinach Loaf with
Béchamel*

Chocolate Brandy Snaps

Brie with Raspberry Coulis and Brioche Toasts

250g (8oz) fresh raspberries

200g (6¹/₂oz) wedge Brie cheese

1 round plain brioche or similar loaf.

8 dried figs, sliced

whole raspberries and mint sprigs for garnish

1 Purée the raspberries in a blender or food processor until smooth, then press through a sieve into a bowl to remove the seeds.

2 Cut the Brie into 4 equal wedges and place on individual plates. Spoon a little raspberry coulis onto each plate.

3 Slice the brioche very finely, toast lightly and add 2 slices to each plate. Garnish each portion to 2 sliced dried figs, 2-3 whole raspberries and a sprig of mint. Serve at once.

Serves 4

Tomato Picasso

Tomato Picasso

8 small tomatoes

60g (2oz) butter

4 eggs, beaten

60ml (2fl oz) single cream

1 tblspn finely snipped chives

¼ avocado, halved, stoned, peeled and finely diced

60ml (2fl oz) soured cream

chives for garnish

1 Cut a thin slice off the top of each tomato. Hollow out the centres, reserving the pulp for use in another dish. Invert the tomatoes on paper towels to drain.

2 Melt the butter in a large frying pan over low heat. Stir in the eggs, single cream, chives and avocado. Gently scramble the eggs but do not overcook.

3 Spoon the mixture into the tomatoes. Top with soured cream and chives. Serve 2 tomatoes per portion.
Serves 4

Brie with Raspberry Coulis and Brioche Toasts

Parmesan-coated Fried Fennel

3 fennel bulbs, trimmed and quartered

185g (6oz) dried breadcrumbs

90g (3oz) Parmesan, grated

2 eggs

salt

oil for frying

1 Place the fennel in a saucepan with cold water to cover. Bring to the boil, lower the heat and simmer for 10 minutes until tender. Drain on paper towels; set aside until cool.

2 Combine the breadcrumbs and cheese in a shallow bowl. Beat the eggs with a pinch of salt in a second shallow bowl. Coat the cooled fennel in egg, then in breadcrumbs, pressing the crumbs on firmly. Stand at room temperature for 15 minutes.

3 Heat oil to a depth of about 2.5cm (1in) in a deep frying pan. Cook the fennel in batches until golden. Drain on paper towels, season with salt and serve.
Serves 4

Spinach Loaf with Béchamel

Spinach Loaf with Béchamel

500g (1lb) fresh or frozen leaf spinach, cooked

2 eggs, lightly beaten

60g (2oz) Parmesan cheese, grated

Béchamel Sauce

75g (2¹/₂oz) butter

30g (1oz) plain flour

600ml (1pt) milk

125ml (4fl oz) double cream

1 Preheat oven to 180°C (350°F/ Gas 4). Drain spinach, pressing out excess liquid; chop leaves finely. Mix with eggs and cheese.

2 Make sauce. Melt 45g (1¹/₂oz) of butter in a saucepan. Stir in flour and cook for 1 minute. Gradually add milk, stirring until sauce boils and thickens.

3 Add half the sauce to spinach mixture; mix well. Spoon the mixture into a greased and lined loaf tin and bake for 30 minutes. Cool in tin for 10 minutes.

4 Reheat remaining sauce. Whisk in remaining butter with cream. Turn out loaf and serve in slices, garnished with a few red pepper slices and a little coriander if liked. Serve with sauce.
Serves 4

Chocolate Brandy Snaps

3 tblspn golden syrup

90g (3oz) butter

60g (2oz) brown sugar

60g (2oz) plain flour

2 tspn cocoa

125g (4oz) milk chocolate, melted

1 Preheat oven to 180°C (350°F/ gas 4). Stir syrup, butter and sugar in a saucepan over gentle heat until butter has melted. Stir in flour and cocoa.

2 Cook 4 brandy snaps at a time: drop scant tablespoons of the mixture onto baking sheets, allowing plenty of room for spreading. Bake for 5-8 minutes.

3 Cool for 1 minute, then lift snaps with a spatula and lay them over a rolling pin to cool and firm up. Drizzle with melted chocolate before serving.
Makes 16-20

Summer Vegetable Pie

Summer Vegetable Pie

2 aubergines, cut into 5mm (¼in) rounds

salt

60ml (2fl oz) oil

1 large onion, chopped

4 courgettes, cut into 5mm (¼in) slices

2 tomatoes, chopped

6 eggs

60ml (2fl oz) milk

60g (2oz) Parmesan cheese, grated

30g (1oz) fresh white breadcrumbs

2 tblspn snipped chives

30g (1oz) Cheddar cheese, grated

1 Spread out aubergine rounds in a colander and sprinkle them with salt. Set aside for 15 minutes to draw out excess liquid, then rinse slices thoroughly. Drain and pat dry on paper towels.

2 Heat oil in a large frying pan. Fry onion for 3 minutes, then add aubergine and courgettes; fry for 5 minutes, stirring occasionally. Add tomatoes and cook for 20 minutes more.

3 In a large mixing bowl, beat eggs with milk. Add Parmesan, breadcrumbs and chives and mix well.

4 Tip contents of frying pan into bowl, stir lightly, then transfer mixture to a lightly greased 23cm (9in) flan dish. Sprinkle Cheddar cheese over top.

5 Bake for 30 minutes. Serve hot or at room temperature.

Serves 4-6

Kitchen Tip

Chives are very easy to grow and are delicious in all egg dishes and snipped into salads. There are several varieties, including one which has a flavour reminiscent of garlic. The easiest way to cut chives is to bunch them together in your hand, then snip them with a pair of kitchen scissors. If fresh chives are not available, substitute freeze-dried chives.

DROP IN FOR DRINKS

One of the least taxing ways of entertaining is to invite friends to drop in for drinks. A couple of interesting cocktails are guaranteed to get any party off to a good start. Prepare a punch, have ready some simple nibbles or canapés, and don't forget alcohol-free beverages for drivers and teetotallers.

Side Car

30ml (1fl oz) cognac

30ml (1fl oz) Cointreau

30ml (1fl oz) freshly squeezed lemon juice

crushed ice

twist of lemon peel

1 Combine the cognac, Cointreau and lemon juice in a cocktail shaker. Add crushed ice. Shake until well combined.

2 Strain into a cocktail glass and serve with a twist of lemon peel.
Serves 1

Buck's Fizz

100ml (3¹/₂fl oz) freshly squeezed orange juice

chilled champagne

Pour the orange juice into a champagne flute. Top up with champagne.
Serves 1

Watermelon Fizz

45g (1¹/₂oz) watermelon, seeded and cubed

4 tblspn crushed ice

125ml (4fl oz) soda water

Purée the water melon with the crushed ice in a blender or food processor. Pour into a tall glass and top up with soda water.
Serves 1

Armagnac Cocktail

750ml (1¹/₄pt) dry white wine

60g (2oz) caster sugar

100ml (3¹/₂fl oz) Armagnac

90ml (3fl oz) freshly squeezed orange juice

chilled champagne

1 Combine the white wine, sugar, Armagnac and orange juice in a large chilled jug. Stir until all the sugar has dissolved.

2 Pour about 60ml (2fl oz) of the mixture into tall champagne flutes. Fill with chilled champagne.
Serves about 15

Bellini

185ml (6fl oz) peach nectar

2 tblspn lemon juice

500ml (16fl oz) champagne

1 Combine the peach nectar and lemon juice in a jug. Divide between 8 champagne flutes.

2 Very slowly, fill each glass with champagne. Stir to combine, add a sprig of mint to the top of each glass and serve.
Serves 8

Kitchen Tip

Crushed – or shaved – ice is used in a variety of cocktails. If you do not have an ice-crusher, wrap cubes in a clean tea-towel and crush them with a meat mallet or rolling pin. Avoid adding whole cubes to a blender or food processor as they may damage the blades.

Bellinis

2 Strain into cocktail glasses. Decorate with orange shreds.
Serves 4

Apricot Brandy Cocktail

1 tblspn apricot brandy

30ml (1fl oz) gin

¹/₂ tspn grenadine

¹/₄ tspn freshly squeezed lemon juice

crushed ice

Combine apricot brandy, gin, grenadine, lemon juice and ice in a cocktail shaker. Shake until well combined. Strain into a cocktail glass.
Serves 1

Kitchen Tip
It is important to use freshly squeezed citrus juices in cocktails; a simple glass juicer is ideal for this purpose.

Pineapple Rum Punch

250ml (8fl oz) white rum

185ml (6fl oz) lemon juice

125g (4oz) caster sugar

125ml (4fl oz) boiling water

500ml (16fl oz) pineapple juice

250ml (8fl oz) orange juice

crushed ice

Combine rum and lemon juice in a large jug. Dissolve sugar in water; add to rum mixture. Stir in pineapple juice and orange juice. Serve in small glasses, over crushed ice.
Serves 8

Apple Ginger Cup

1 litre (1³/₄pt) apple juice

3 tblspn finely chopped crystallized ginger

1 tblspn grenadine

Combine all the ingredients in a blender or food processor. Process until smooth. Serve in tall glasses.
Serves 4

Negroni

Iced Citrus Tea

4 Orange Pekoe tea bags

600ml (1pt) boiling water

125ml (4fl oz) freshly squeezed lemon juice

75g (2¹/₂oz) caster sugar

1.2 litres (2pt) bottled lemonade, chilled

1 orange, thinly sliced

8 mint sprigs

1 Place tea bags in a heatproof jug. Boil 500ml (16fl oz) of water, pour it into jug and infuse for 5 minutes; remove tea bags. Add lemon juice and let liquid cool.

2 Put remaining water in a small saucepan. Add sugar. Stir over low heat until all the sugar has dissolved. Boil without stirring for 3 minutes. When cool, stir syrup into cold tea mixture. Refrigerate for at least 2 hours until ready to serve.

3 Fill glasses half full with the tea mixture. Top up with chilled lemonade. Float a thin slice of orange on each drink and decorate with a sprig of mint.
Serves 8

Negroni

Despite its pretty appearance, this cocktail packs a powerful punch.

125ml (4fl oz) gin

125ml (4fl oz) Campari

125ml (4fl oz) dry vermouth

crushed ice

shredded orange peel

1 Combine gin, Campari and vermouth in a cocktail shaker. Add crushed ice. Shake until well combined.

Orange Champagne

This is a variation on Buck's Fizz.

250ml (8fl oz) freshly squeezed orange juice

125ml (4fl oz) Cointreau

1 tblspn caster sugar

1 bottle chilled champagne

1 Combine the orange juice, Cointreau and sugar in a large jug. Stir until all the sugar has dissolved.

2 Divide mixture between 8 champagne flutes. Top up with chilled champagne.
Serves 8

Florida Cocktail

30ml (1fl oz) Cointreau

30ml (1fl oz) gin

1 tblspn freshly squeezed orange juice

ice cubes

Combine Cointreau, gin, orange juice and ice cubes in a shaker. Shake until well combined. Strain into a cocktail glass.
Serves 1

Raspberries Vodka

Flavoured vodkas are extremely popular – fruits, herbs and even aromatic grasses are used to great effect. This richly coloured drink owes its flavour to raspberries.

125g (4oz) fresh raspberries

250ml (8fl oz) vodka

1 Combine raspberries and vodka in a perfectly clean bottle or screwtop jar. Close tightly.

2 Refrigerate for 3 days, shaking jar or bottle daily.

3 Strain mixture through a fine sieve into a jug. Divide between 6 glasses.
Serves 6

Variation
For a long drink, top Raspberries Vodka with soda water, sparkling mineral water or tonic water.

Fruit Cooler

This is a good choice for patio parties or picnics.

750ml (1¼pt) unsweetened pineapple juice

250ml (8fl oz) freshly squeezed lemon juice

2 litres (3½pt) freshly squeezed orange juice

ice cubes

blackcurrant syrup

1 Combine fruit juices in a large jug. Cover and refrigerate for at least 2 hours or until well chilled and ready to serve.

2 To serve, half fill 12 tall glasses with ice cubes. Drizzle a little blackcurrant syrup over each and fill up with fruit juice mixture.
Serves 12

Hot Drambuie

250ml (8fl oz) Drambuie

4 tblspn freshly squeezed lemon juice

4 thin lemon slices

4 thin orange slices

500ml (16fl oz) boiling water

4 cinnamon sticks

1 Heat 4 mugs by filling them with boiling water, leaving them to stand for a few minutes, then draining and drying them swiftly.

2 Divide Drambuie between the mugs. Add 1 tablespoon lemon juice to each, with 1 slice each of lemon and orange.

3 Pour 125ml (4fl oz) boiling water into each mug. Add cinnamon sticks as stirrers. Serve at once.
Serves 4

Raspberries Vodka

Hot 'n' Frothy Cocktail

Hot 'n' Frothy Cocktail

375ml (12fl oz) milk

60ml (2fl oz) Cointreau

2 tblspn cognac

ground cinnamon to serve

1 Heat the milk in a saucepan to just below boiling point. Pour into a blender and blend until frothy.

2 Add the Cointreau and cognac and blend until combined. Pour into 4 heat-resistant glasses, sprinkle with cinnamon and serve.
Serves 4

Frosty Grape

250g (8oz) seedless green grapes, frozen

500ml (16fl oz) white grape juice

185g (6oz) honeydew melon, roughly chopped

small bunches of grapes to serve

Combine the grapes, grape juice and melon in a blender or food processor. Process until smooth and frosty. Pour into chilled glasses. Decorate each glass with a tiny bunch of seedless green grapes and serve at once.
Serves 6

Campari and Soda

Campari and Soda

125ml (4fl oz) Campari

250ml (8fl oz) soda water

orange peel for decoration

Divide Campari between 2 cocktail glasses. Fill with soda. Add ice to each glass and decorate with a strip of orange peel.
Serves 2

Rum-Whisky Eggnog

Enliven after-theatre parties with this deceptively mild-tasting drink. Use fresh eggs from a reputable source.

18 eggs, separated

500g (1lb) caster sugar

2 litres (3¹/2pt) milk

1 bottle whisky

375ml (12fl oz) dark rum

750ml (1¹/4pt) single cream

nutmeg

1 Using a hand-held electric mixer, beat the egg yolks with the sugar in a large mixing bowl until thick and pale. Spoon into a large punch bowl. Stir in the milk, whisky and rum.

2 In a separate bowl, beat the cream to soft peaks. Fold into the mixture in the punch bowl.

3 Beat the egg whites in 2-3 batches in a grease-free bowl until stiff. Add to the punch bowl and fold in evenly. Grate plenty of nutmeg over the top of the eggnog and stir in well.

4 Cover the bowl closely and refrigerate until ready to serve.
Serves about 20

Kitchen Tip
Freshly grated nutmeg is essential for this eggnog and is a delicious addition to numerous other dishes, including white sauces, stewed fruit and meatloaves. Keep a nutmeg grater near the hob and clean it regularly with a small child's toothbrush kept especially for the purpose.

COME AGAIN

Cooking for friends gives you licence to throw caution – and calories – to the winds. The desserts in this chapter include a creamy shortcake, a rich brandy pecan pie and a featherlight Pavlova, all guaranteed to ensure your guests come back for more!

Country Apple Flan

Pastry

250g (8oz) plain flour

1/4 tspn salt

30g (1oz) butter

1 tspn easy blend dried yeast

90-125ml (3-4fl oz) warm water

Filling

1kg (2lb) Bramley apples, peeled and thinly sliced

90g (3oz) caster sugar

3 tblspn orange marmalade

2 tblspn soft brown sugar

2 tspn ground cinnamon

1 Combine flour and salt in a mixing bowl. Rub in butter, then stir in yeast. Add enough warm water to make a soft dough.

2 Knead dough on a floured surface for about 5 minutes or until smooth and elastic. Place in a large bowl, cover and set aside in a warm place for 1 hour.

3 Meanwhile cook apples in large saucepan with caster sugar and a little water. As soon as apples soften, but before they lose their shape, remove half of them from pan and set aside. Cook remaining apples to a purée; drain and stir.

4 Preheat oven to 180°C (350°F/ Gas 4). Roll out dough on a floured surface to fit a lightly greased 25cm (10in) flan dish. Spread base with marmalade and spread the apple purée on top.

5 Arrange reserved apple slices in concentric rings on top of the apple purée. Mix brown sugar and cinnamon together and sprinkle over apples.

6 Bake flan for 20-30 minutes or until pastry is well risen and golden. Serve warm.
Serves 8-12

Cherry Hazelnut Meringue Torte

4 egg whites

250g (8oz) caster sugar

125g (4oz) hazelnuts, ground

90g (3oz) cherry jam

375ml (12fl oz) double cream, whipped

2 x 425g (15oz) cans black cherries, drained

1 Preheat oven to 150°C (300°F/ Gas 2). Beat egg whites in a grease-free bowl until soft peaks form. Gradually add sugar, beating constantly until meringue is stiff.

2 Fold hazelnuts into meringue. Spread mixture evenly over base of two 23cm (9in) cake tins lined with greased baking parchment. Bake for 1 hour. Cool, then remove from tins and transfer one meringue to a serving plate.

3 Spread meringue with cherry jam and top with half the whipped cream. Set aside about 24 cherries for decoration; arrange rest on top of cream. Top with the second meringue. Decorate torte with remaining cream and cherries.
Serves 8

Country Apple Flan

Berry Shortcake

155g (5oz) plain flour

45g (1½oz) self-raising flour

155g (5oz) chilled butter, cubed

2 tblspn caster sugar

milk, see method

Filling

185g (6oz) strawberries, hulled and halved

125g (4oz) raspberries, hulled

125g (4oz) blueberries or drained canned blackcurrants

3 tblspn raspberry liqueur

Glaze

125g (4oz) raspberry jam

60g (2oz) caster sugar

2 tblspn lemon juice

1 tspn gelatine dissolved in 2 tblspn water

1 Make shortcake. Mix flours in a large bowl. Rub in butter until mixture resembles fine breadcrumbs, then add sugar. Stir in just enough milk to bind dough. Roll into a ball, wrap closely and chill for 30 minutes.

2 Preheat oven to 180°C (350°F/ Gas 4). Roll out dough on a lightly floured surface and line a 23cm (9in) loose-based flan dish. The shortcake dough should be quite thick. Fill pie shell with crumpled foil. Bake for 20-25 minutes, until golden brown. Remove foil and cool.

3 Gently toss berries, with the currants if using, in a bowl with liqueur. Set aside for 1 hour. Strain, reserving liquid, and arrange berries in shortcake shell.

4 To make glaze, heat jam, sugar, lemon juice, gelatine and reserved berry liquid in a saucepan, stirring until sugar and gelatine have dissolved. Bring to boil, lower heat and simmer for 3 minutes.

5 Brush glaze over berries. Allow to cool and set before serving.
Serves 6-8

Brandy Pecan Pie

315g (10oz) plain flour

375g (12oz) chilled butter

1 tblspn caster sugar

250g (8oz) soft brown sugar

375g (12oz) golden syrup

4 eggs, beaten

1 tspn vanilla essence

2 tblspn brandy

185g (6oz) pecan nuts

1 Put flour in a large bowl. Cube 250g (8oz) of butter and rub it into flour until mixture resembles breadcrumbs; stir in caster sugar. Add just enough iced water to bind dough. Roll out and line a 25cm (10in) pie dish.

2 Preheat oven to 190°C (375°F/ Gas 5). Fill pie shell with crumpled foil and bake for 10 minutes. Remove foil.

3 Heat brown sugar, syrup and remaining butter in a saucepan, stirring until sugar has dissolved. Cool slightly.

4 Stir eggs, vanilla and brandy into syrup mixture. Arrange pecans in concentric circles on the base of pie shell pressing them lightly into pastry. Pour in filling. Bake for 45 minutes. Serve cold, with cream, if liked.
Serves 8

Chocolate Cream Dream Cake

2 x 200g (6½oz) bars chocolate, broken into squares

600ml (1pt) double cream

1 tspn vanilla essence

250ml (8fl oz) strong black coffee

4 tblspn orange-flavoured liqueur

3 packets sponge fingers (about 72)

whipped cream and chocolate curls to decorate

1 Melt chocolate in a heatproof bowl over hot water. Cool slightly. In a separate bowl, beat double cream with vanilla until thick. Stir in chocolate, mixing well.

2 Mix the coffee and liqueur in a shallow bowl. Line a 23cm (9in) square cake tin with cling film, overlapping the edges. Arrange a layer of sponge fingers on the bottom, dipping each sponge finger in the coffee mixture before fitting it into place. Cover with half chocolate mixture, then another layer of sponge fingers. Top with remaining chocolate mixture and sponge fingers. Cover and freeze until firm.

3 To serve, invert frozen cake on a platter; remove cling film. When thawed, decorate with whipped cream and chocolate curls.
Serves 20

Passionfruit Pavlova

6 egg whites

pinch cream of tartar

2 tspn cornflour

250g (8oz) caster sugar

300ml (10fl oz) double cream, whipped

4 passionfruit

1 tblspn snipped fresh mint

1 Preheat oven to 140°C (275°F/ Gas 1). Using a hand-held electric mixer, beat egg whites in a grease-free bowl until glossy. Combine cream of tartar, cornflour and sugar and gradually add to egg whites, beating constantly until stiff.

2 Grease a 23cm (9in) springform cake tin and base line with baking parchment. Dust with cornflour.

3 Spoon meringue into tin and spread out evenly. Bake for 1½ hours. Turn off oven and leave door ajar until meringue is cool. Transfer meringue to a serving plate, top with whipped cream, passionfruit pulp and mint and serve.
Serves 6-8

Apricot Meringue Dacquoise

The meringues and apricot purée may be prepared in advance and the dessert assembled just before serving.

3 egg whites

185g (6oz) caster sugar

60g (2oz) ground almonds

1 tblspn plain flour

125g (4oz) dried apricots

185ml (6fl oz) water

2 tblspn golden granulated sugar

2 tspn grated lemon rind

2 tblspn lemon juice

375ml (12fl oz) double cream, whipped

30g (1oz) dark chocolate, grated

4 glacé apricots, cut into strips, for decoration

1 Preheat oven to 140°C (275°F/ Gas 1). Beat egg whites in a grease-free bowl until soft peaks form, then gradually add caster sugar, beating constantly. Stir in almonds and flour. Divide mixture between three greased 23cm (9in) springform cake tins, lined with baking parchment. Bake for 1 hour. Cool, then remove layers from tins.

2 Combine apricots, water, sugar, lemon rind and juice in a saucepan. Bring to boil, lower heat and simmer for 15 minutes or until apricots are tender. Purée in a blender or food processor; cool.

3 Place a meringue layer on a serving plate. Spread with half the apricot purée, then with one third of the whipped cream. Top with a second meringue. Add rest of purée and half remaining cream. Fit final meringue in place and use remaining cream to decorate top and sides of dacquoise. Decorate with grated chocolate and glacé apricot strips.

Serves 8-12

Chocolate Truffles

375ml (12fl oz) double cream

220g (7oz) bittersweet chocolate, finely grated

cocoa, see method

1 Pour cream into a saucepan. Bring to boil slowly, then boil, stirring constantly, until cream has reduced by half.

2 Remove pan from heat and add chocolate. Stir until smooth. Pour mixture into a shallow dish and refrigerate for about 5 hours or until firm.

3 Form heaped teaspoons of the mixture into balls; roll in cocoa until well coated. Place on a platter, cover and refrigerate until ready to serve.

Makes about 24

Cheese Platter

315g (10oz) Camembert

315g (10oz) Cheddar

250g (8oz) cheese with fruit, such as apricot roule

200g (6¹/₂oz) Stilton

125g (4oz) fresh dates

1 pear, halved, cored and sliced

1 mandarin, peeled and segmented

small neat bread slices or water biscuits to serve

Have cheese at room temperature. Arrange it on a suitable board, with dates, pear slices and mandarin segments. Serve with bread or biscuits.

Serves 4

Kitchen Tip
Fan the pear out as suggested for Pear and Smoked Chicken Salad (page 6), if liked.

Cheese Platter

USEFUL INFORMATION

Length

Centimetres	Inches	Centimetres	Inches
0.5 (5mm)	$1/4$	18	7
1	$1/2$	20	8
2	$3/4$	23	9
2.5	1	25	10
4	$1^1/2$	30	12
5	2	35	14
6	$2^1/2$	40	16
7.5	3	45	18
10	4	50	20
15	6	NB: 1cm = 10mm	

Metric/Imperial Conversion Chart
Mass (Weight)
(Approximate conversions for cookery purposes)

Metric	Imperial	Metric	Imperial
15g	$1/2$oz	315g	10oz
30g	1oz	350g	11oz
60g	2oz	375g	12oz ($3/4$lb)
90g	3oz	410g	13oz
125g	4oz ($1/4$lb)	440g	14oz
155g	5oz	470g	15oz
185g	6oz	500g (0.5kg)	16oz (1lb)
220g	7oz	750g	24oz ($1^1/2$lb)
250g	8oz ($1/2$lb)	1000g (1kg)	32oz (2lb)
280g	9oz	1500 (1.5kg)	3lb

Metric Spoon Sizes

$1/4$ teaspoon	= 1.25ml
$1/2$ teaspoon	= 2.5ml
1 teaspoon	= 5ml
1 tablespoon	=15ml

Liquids

Metric	Imperial
30ml	1fl oz
60ml	2fl oz
90ml	3fl oz
125ml	4fl oz
155ml	5fl oz ($1/4$pt)
185ml	6fl oz
250ml	8fl oz
500ml	16fl oz
600ml	20fl oz (1pt)
750ml	$1^1/4$pt
1 litre	$1^3/4$pt
1.2 litres	2pt
1.5 litres	$2^1/2$pt
1.8 litres	3pt
2 litres	$3^1/2$pt
2.5 litres	4pt

Index

Apple Ginger Cup	38	Fettucine Alfredo	19	Prawns with Garlic and	
Apricot Brandy Cocktail	38	Florida Cocktail	39	Rosemary	11
Apricot Chicken	16	Frosty Grape	40	Quick Nasi Goreng	13
Apricot Meringue Dacquoise	46	Fruit Cooler	39	Radicchio with Peas	18
Armagnac Cocktail	36	Glazed Butternut Squash	26	Raspberries Vodka	39
Basil-scented Prawn Skewers	28	Glazed Ham and Sausagemeat		Ratatouille Crumble	25
Beetroot and Carrot Salad	31	Loaf	11	Risotto with Cheese and	
Bellini	36	Glazed Turnips and Carrots	23	Pinenuts	12
Berries and Mascarpone	23	Green Beans with Sesame		Risotto with Smoked Salmon	12
Berry Shortcake	44	Seeds	25	Rosemary Crispy Potatoes	22
Brandy Pecan Pie	44	Hot 'n' Frothy Cocktail	40	Rum-Whisky Eggnog	41
Brie with Raspberry Coulis		Hot Drambuie	39	Scallop Soup with Vermouth	
and Brioche Toasts	32	Iced Citrus Tea	38	and Lime	3
Buck's Fizz	36	Italian Mussel Soup	3	Seafood Pot Pie	14
Campari and Soda	41	Kiwi Fruit Sorbet	27	Seafood Terrine	7
Cheese Platter	46	Lamb and Mango Skewers	28	Side Car	36
Cheesy Rice Ring with Garlic		Lamb in Red Wine	22	Smoked Salmon Soup	4
Vegetables	13	Lemon Sole Ragout	15	Spanish Seafood Casserole	14
Cherry Hazelnut Meringue Torte	42	Linguine with Prawns and Olives	18	Spinach Loaf with Béchamel	34
Chicken and Mushroom Parcels	8	Loin of Lamb with Prune		Spinach Soup with Sausage	
Chicken Breasts with Lemon		Pinenut Stuffing	24	Meatballs	5
and Brandy	8	Mozzarella Ham Parcels	5	Steak and Courgette Burgers	28
Chocolate Brandy Snaps	34	Negroni	38	Summer Vegetable Pie	35
Chocolate Cream Dream Cake	44	Orange Champagne	39	Tomato Picasso	33
Chocolate Truffles	46	Orange Jellies with Fresh Fruit	26	Tomato Pilaf	12
Cold Garlic Prawns with Avocado	6	Orange-scented Oxtail Stew	16	Warm Mussel Salad with	
Country Apple Flan	42	Parmesan-coated Fried Fennel	33	Walnut Dressing	21
Crisp Cheese Pitta Wedges	31	Passionfruit Pavlova	44	Watercress Soup	4
Crispy Fantail Potatoes	26	Pear and Smoked Chicken Salad	6	Watermelon Fizz	36
Fennel with Ham	16	Peppered Chicken Breast Fillets	8	Wholemeal Pasta with	
		Pineapple Rum Punch	38	Mushrooms and Sun-dried	
		Pork and Mushroom Casserole	16	Tomatoes	19
		Pork with Apple Cider Sauce	16	Winter Vegetable Soup	4

Editorial Coordination: Merehurst Limited
Cookery Editor: Jenni Fleetwood
Editorial Assistant: Sheridan Packer
Production Managers: Sheridan Carter, Anna Maguire
Layout and Finished Art: Stephen Joseph
Cover Photography: Clive Streeter
Cover Design: Maggie Aldred
Cover Home Economist: Kathy Man
Cover Stylist: Hilary Guy

Published by J.B. Fairfax Press Pty Limited
80-82 McLachlan Avenue
Rushcutters Bay 2011
A.C.N. 003 738 430

Formatted by J. B. Fairfax Press Pty Limited
Printed by Toppan Printing Co, Singapore

JBFP 345 A/UK
Includes Index
ISBN 1 86343 116 0 (set)
ISBN 1 86343 183 7

Distribution and Sales Enquiries
Australia: J.B. Fairfax Press Pty Limited
Ph: (02) 361 6366 Fax: (02) 360 6262
United Kingdom: J.B. Fairfax Press Pty Limited
Ph: (0933) 402330 Fax: (0933) 402234